BRENDA SHAUGHNESSY

Interior
with Sudden Joy

BRENDA SHAUGHNESSY was raised in California and is a graduate of Columbia University's writing program. She lives in New York City.

Interior

with Sudden Joy

INTERIOR

WITH SUDDEN JOY

BRENDA

SHAUGHNESSY

[*Farrar, Straus and Giroux, New York*]

Farrar, Straus and Giroux
19 Union Square West, New York 10003

Copyright © 1999 by Brenda Shaughnessy
All rights reserved
Distributed in Canada by Douglas & McIntyre Ltd.
Printed in the United States of America
Designed by Cynthia Krupat
First published in 1999 by Farrar, Straus and Giroux
First paperback edition, 2000

Library of Congress Cataloging-in-Publication Data
Shaughnessy, Brenda, 1970–
    Interior with sudden joy / Brenda Shaughnessy. — 1st ed.
    p. cm.
    ISBN 0-374-52698-2 (pbk.)
    I. Title.
    PS3569.H353I55   1999
    811'.54—dc21   *98-50010*

Contents

[*I*]

Synesthesia

Still Life, with Gloxinia

I will make something of you both pigment
and insecticide. Something natural,
even red, like serviceberries.
Which a cloister of young Benedictine
nuns, in exile and drought,
found and brilliantly crushed
into a blessed moxie wine.
With terrible pride, with gloxinia,
the slipper-shaped flower, served
it bitter and staining in the chalice.
By evening chapel, habits thrown up
and still, their insides found all blue,
as suspected. I am cold now and I cannot
paint or move you.

Letter to the Crevice Novice

I wanted nothing. I am not a stray mule
& gaudy caravan pulling a big skirt,
open legs, a head of wire.

I want singers to shear your eye from the flocking
of my city of superior grammar & wincing.
To keep you blind, my alabaster scourge.

It must be a Love, this crackpot of heart,
my sterling & cashmere & no money.
You my fat bad fricassee, cough of a candle.

Through snow, my little weather, you are gone
through the cravesty turnstile
to my other kind of homemaking.

I've always been home outside.
Night likes me. Vampiring I would have killed
all I loved & kept all our lives

for centuries, crypt-crock. Love was death
enough. How deep is the Mariana Trench?
For the crevice novice, anything more

than six feet is bottomfeeding. Deeper
than that, the proxy eros is tricking us
good: tight No-love-you's in a tongue

thicker than water. Bluer too.

Fetish: The Historical Orphan

Czarina! Tell me you're not giving up the rogue
red rule for a cottage edged with timothy and vague
whortleroot. Make room for me in your scullery,

strange queen of Siber with your hand stroking the back
of Mongolia. It is too low a land and the dear
intima of your delicate organs will brush

desperately against your blue inner skin.
I would volunteer myself, if I weren't such a trollop
on queue for the strappado. In my heart,

I'm a candidate for the spoon of strychnine
in my tea. I would choose that, if your well-missed
wonderland of punishment were here.

But it's not. You have left me to the rack, which
I will accommodate. My journalbox of love letters
to you is bursting. Someday my family will slide

out around these censors, scoundrels, and send my
devotions, like a sea of raving quillfish, an imbroglio
of plainstone and flogging, to you in your exile.

May Mother Russia lie burnt inside your shepherdess
skirt. May your meager nest be filled with peahen
as good a meal as I have been for your uniformed surrogates.

Someday may your icy love know the affliction
of the abandoned, of the sexual underchild: cyclopia,
a fusing of the retinas, to see yourself as I see you.

Lure, Lapse

There is no style in sleep,
only the sense of nethers startled
up from the supple interior.

Guarded handsomely, I am awake
(for a baker of course in love
with a painter will mix too hard)

and preening in the lord-loud and ecstatic doubt
purchased from all last nude cringing.

Dull bronze cowbells for hands
is what I want.

The serious honeycomb leaking,
I would streak you with yellow bruises.
Your garland, my shaky lamb,

we are close in this
slow evening gown,

we are growing down,
our winter-slung bodies fooled
and necklaced with furious morning.

Jouissance

Your phantoms hang neatly from skyhooks,
ready to be veils, ready to disembody you.

You have shelled yourself of this curved room
and the smell is of burnt door,

slackbelly, hot. It is an abattoir,
lacking its usual firmness.

Your ordinary sweet kinesis, peevish
in the crumble and whetstone of your body.

And so you go. Every city has a place called the Roxy.
Go. To keep from the quicksand of this:

Unbearable curl. Tender leviathan in the last
window, crimson facing west.

How could you? You are Gundella.
You are anyone's Maria.

Electric to perishing, your more auxiliary lovers,
like pralines or quaaludes, cannot touch you.

No teasing or lockjaw. Caustic. All of you, even shadow,
must be bull's-eye. Your shaggy, skeptical

quasar has died the way Andromeda dies:
so very late at night. You are disenchanted.

You are all rain-collected, in a butterfish sac
opaque and draining.

The description of this you hold under
like a genius in dark water.

Vapor through Various Satins

I have been so dirty
in each place you've looked

my body has absorbed
the light, the iris stain,

and marked me. Mud.
Bruise. Calendar of salt

and faith. I will try,
in the sun and in lesser

fire, to blot this slur, flaw
discolored, with the speckled

cloth of near origin: our
bedclothes, those trophies

fringed flat and holy. Such
a ripe display. Starling,

skillbreast, swathed too
clean and brief-handed,

fall over yourself leaving,
your hinged, your blurred

silhouette etched, rising
more visible, more liquid.

Afterlife, Her Empty Dress

I lie quiet among my possible suits,
feet to head, feet to head.
Blue, black, white, red.

I am grim at the waist, squandered
through the legs. Watch
with a turned-in face.

Lie with a design on my back, a spade
in clover. Been given
a flat of stone to line

my fortress, and a curtain of privacy
for your old sweet water.
Can you see me

on the other side of the jumpy garden
coiled out to you?
Blind as a wedding,

so white you're blue. Little fog queen,
without a corpse,
I take you peeled

too bright. I throw you starved of air.
I kiss you still warm,
colored with ash.

I leave you under a cloud, but I carve
you in night, that finer
edge, the old arc of your hand.

What's Uncanny

is the body's wiry edge singed & dried,
touched at last by the curious

gloves of the question guard.
Too much choreography.

Hamstrings, half edible & music,
stretched like catgut, the sad-animal pull.

Our knees two peculiar systems
of locking, of looking. Too little dance.

Compulsion is always narcissism:
I miss you, admit it.

I'm gifted, I give in. I give you
all my old synesthetic fire.

Loved-body smoke is terribly popular
in dry neighborhoods,

and our lungs are succulents. We share
this loss of breathing. Listen for it.

Transpassional

Perfection is the campsite for those who have stopped halfway.
I've melted my silver for you.

Belonging is invisible: this can be seen at the proper distance.
I've burned my blue curtains

and spent myself on an intricate openwork of razor wire, to cut
skylights for the honeybees in webs.

I'm living alone in a kind of cube which is barely electric, the hot
plate blows the tiny fuse

but I have noodles and wine and a nice singing voice. If you
came back I could make you

a necklace. The small planets drop by every few months, slivered;
the big ones never and never

do I feel abandoned. Belonging is invisible: I, on the other hand,
am merely shielding.

Swell

Svelte with eventual sex, who could help
but gorge herself on low violet leaning everywhere?

The shine and shifting slate of the sky murmurs
its irresistible confession: *I am more than blue*

if you are the violent imprint. I am swollen,
vexed endlessly and only
finite against your bodies.

This slim stalk of silhouette slides via nimbus
down the eyelights without a skirmish.
Glossy with sly undoing, blisterlike.

We are disheveled, though too
skeptical to abandon our dimpled limbs

and fill the insides of slips with mere
threat and strop of thunderpeal.

We toss freely with fever this mirror
desilvered. And break into rain upon
finding such umber yielding of frost to febris.

This strumpet muscle under your breast describing
you minutely, *Volupt, volupt.*

Dear Gonglya,

The most inscrutable beautiful names in this world
always do sound like diseases.
It is because they are *engorged.*
G., I am a fool.
What we feel in the solar plexus wrecks us.
Halfway squatting on a crate where feeling happened. Caresses.

You know corporeal gifts besmirch thieves like me.
But she plucks a feather and my steam escapes.
                              We're awake
each night at pennymoon and we micro and necro.
I can't stop. But love and what-all:
the uncomfortable position of telling the truth,
like the lotus, can't be held long.
                              If she knew would she
just take all her favors from my marmalade
vessel and chuck them back
into the endless reversible garment which is my life—
                              an astonishing vanishing.
G., I know this letter is like a slice of elevator accident.
As smart folk would say,
"Everything is only Nothing's Truck."

I would revise it and say that everything is only nothing, truncated.

Love,

Your Igor

I am calling to wish you well. I am calling because I want to change something I said. A year ago you asked me three questions. I thought you were asking my birthday wishes and answered all wrong. If you remember (if I know you you'll pretend you don't) I answered:

1) No. I have always been homely.
2) Yes. I believe you have always been too lovely for anyone to bear.
3) Silk. It is not always expensive, and it is impossible to tear.

It's my birthday again and because I am cleverer now I can answer you with more nerve. But because I am still me I am pitiless enough to have your number and to call you with this excuse to let you know I am still alive (I won't push it by telling you that I am wonderful).

1) Yes. Thank you.
2) No. I found a most repulsive photo.
3) Same. Though I don't think of you, still it's a near-perfect heat. And so dear when ruined.

Rise

I can't believe you've come back,
like the train I missed so badly, barely,
which stopped & returned for me. It scared me,
humming backwards along the track.

I rise to make a supper succulent
for the cut of your mouth, your bite of wine
so sharp, you remember you were mine.
You may resist, you will relent.

At home in fire, desire is bread
whose flour, water, salt and yeast,
not yet confused, are still, at least,
in the soil, the sea, the mine, the dead.

I have all I longed for, you
in pleasure. You missed me, your body swelling.
Once more, you lie with me, smelling
of almonds, as the poisoned do.

Fortune

Luck today will be skill tomorrow. If only your fear
held now gorgeous in its white cotton frock
could become small and frayed in the next millennia.

Be brown and blowsy and on the ledge instead. Used
and fueling, a succubus cannot ruin what she pulls
on her tricky leash: dread's body, desire's body.

If terror bent double could thicken into a frenzy
for the last flushed basket of windfalls
that arms October, could you really wander

forever in that shelter? Are wondering and losing
the same? If you ply me now all pure-voiced,
with some sepia trinket from your big box of ducks,

could I sculpt this cold knowledge into the fresh
hot fruit swinging in next summer's
branches, slimsy in rain, saturated

in the pear-flustered color closed in your eyes?
This bleary, fragile calendar: Your disbelief,
your loveable haunting. How clever you are

tomorrow. The expert veils around your face, scarlet
fabric woven by apprentices whose fingers
are sad and large with the work of beginning.

Glossary
(of the body, performed in absentia)

Appendix A: Irregular Verbs

Nursing:
> The milk won the meat
> and the feet cheered.

Writing:
> To bones, fat is only fog.

Whispering:
(see also *Secreting*)
> Speckles furious at dots,
> and all of them drunk in expensive boxes.

Nervous Throbbing:
> The softest eggs, trembling for wax paper,
> but a song would do.

Praying:
> Peculiar remarks from a peripheral cousin.

Lying:
> (down) When doing, no matter what else,
>   one cannot be the worst off in the world.

(little, white) Pressed essence of ham and corkboard.

Dreaming:
> What is made from scrap sapphire
> found lying around one's basement?

Begrudging:
> A counterfeit fit.

Forgetting:
> Boil feelers till soft, scrape off scorched
> bits, put back in head.

Trying:
> I can never tell the truly gray heart, distracted as I am
> by what is red about it.

Sexing:
> Narrative Inclusion.

Writing:
> The juice knife had its art cut, and ran.
> (Example: I am mad at you.)

Twisting:
> (esp. ankle) Having pink, secure in the honey-only club,
> but too dark to see by the moon so, insulted, rust.

Fingering:
 Arms disarmed and explaining themselves.

Thinking:
 Such truths are only perversions of the perfected false.
 Plucked from the drink of a drunk heart.

Tonguing:
(see also *Writing*)
 Enormous language smears your place.

Dark Church

of Hands

Middle

The last minutes of your life
you spend dyeing wisteria.

A slashing
in slanted alley light.

Born in the middle of the parting, groping
in with two beautiful eyes on your arm,

the first minutes of your life
you spend loving your feet backwards.

Broken house, summer house,
the middle voice of fish.

Without this voice, you will spend all winter
blackening into bits.

Your One Good Dress

should never be light. That kind of thing feels
like a hundred shiny-headed waifs backlit
and skeletal, approaching. Dripping and in
unison, murmuring, "We *are* you."

No. And the red dress (think about it,
redress) is all neckhole. The brown
is a big wet beard with, of course, a backslit.
You're only as sick as your secrets.

There is an argument for the dull-chic,
the dirty olive and the Cinderelly. But those
who exhort it are only part of the conspiracy:
"Shimmer, shmimmer," they'll say. "Lush, shmush."

Do not listen. It's a part of the anti-obvious
movement and it's sheer matricide. Ask your mum.
It would kill her if you were ewe gee el why.
And is it a crime to wonder, am I. In the dark a dare,

Am I now. You put on your Niña, your Pinta, your
Santa María. Make it simple to last your whole
life long. Make it black. Glassy or deep.
Your body is opium and you are its only true smoker.

This black dress is your one good dress.
Bury your children in it. Visit your pokey
hometown friends in it. Go missing for days.
Taking it off never matters. That just wears you down.

Your Name on It

Let this one clear square of thought be just
like a room you could come to in. An attic room,
after you've swiveled over to the wrecked
corner of the champagne. After you

hand-rolled cigarettes and ass and sold
your best midnight speech to a slick jack
of clubs. For a stingy cut: a wet, bony
kiss. You have nothing left to say

and nothing to say it with. Mouths,
whole faces even, have been pilfered
in prettier ways. For everyone who ever
looked at you and thought *that one thinks*

its so damn easy, you don't have to look
back at them. Ha! It is easy. This room
has no mirror, no leap-leer to strain
or stylize the fuzz of your body through

the razor of your eye. This room is dark,
and high. If you spit out the window
you could kill a bug. There's the document.
There's always the window, your signature.

Simulacra

Having no effect on myself,
a mirror erases me. My own touch

feels like porn in a glass case
in a museum still being designed.

Eating eats me. Walking dusts me.
Holding reminds me of fishes and the looming

reelings I had when I caught one,
then lost it or scaled it down to size.

My size. Nothing became of it,
and nothing is quite

so becoming on me. I find my hide
flaking off on the eye chair:

This is what I used to play myself with.
This is what I used to see the feel.

Rosarium

Ardent goodwife of a bad fisherman, I am blessed
with a fiery talent, given a generous
length of sewing silk, privacy

and a picture tinted almost obscene with bog violet,
framed and neutered on the flustered
vanity table. Never enter

my chambers, the dark church of hands. I climb
the trellis of my own skeleton, alone
and blooming, sexennial.

All is only my heat, my pierced and rushing Madonna
of sheepweed, my beloved secret body
lustrous and raped in the mirror.

The mirror, strong as a tapestry needle, and through
this eye I fit, smaller, deeper, inside.

Lacquer

I found my mother's diary,
an indigo sack of silk and ink.
I read it. The words in Japanese
but the characters as American
as a girl of fashionable twelve
bearing an amnesia so dense
she could never drag it
out into the yard.

I couldn't tell you what
my mother's diary said.
That is private.
She would never tell me
that living always
with a husband's
language is like having
birthmarks on the pancreas.
Or that failing to persuade
daughters to sing open
her far invisible house
was an insomniac's mudwell,
an alien pox in the polished dark.

Epithalament

Other weddings are so shrewd on the sofa, short
and baffled, bassett-legged. All things

knuckled, I have no winter left, in my sore rememory,
to melt down for drinking water. Shrunk down.

Your wedding slides the way wiry dark hairs do, down
a swimming pool drain. So I am drained.

Sincerely. I wish you every chapped bird on this
pilgrimage to hold your hem up from the dust.

Dust is plural: infinite dust. I will sink in the sun,
I will crawl towards the heavy drawing

and design the curtains in the room
of never marrying you. Because it is a sinking,

because today's perfect weather is a later life's
smut. This soiled future unplans love.

I keep unplanning the same Sunday. Leg
and flower, breeze and terrier, I have no garden

and couldn't be happier. Please, don't lose me
here. I am sorry my clutch is all

tendon and no discipline: the heart is a severed
kind of muscle and alone.

I can hear yours in your room. I hear mine
in another room. In another's.

Thirteenth Summer

Who is twelve? Not you, in absolute skirt,
and sweet on treasures twisted out
from underneath the pokeweed and plywood.

Someone has promised you sticky canyon jewels,
and then showed you where to put your hands,
saying, *It's like peeling the sky.*

And suddenly in your nervous uncle's
fuchsia garden your life has the smell
of an old bone corset you've never seen.

In your own miniature Illinois, the nightsworth
of ever-early trains runs you ragged with wool
insomnia, squandered earthquake.

Slowly, in a tight dress, cheating at truth
or dare, a quick liquid has stolen its rival,
heat, from your round body as you cross into sleep.

Starting Here and Going Back

Stranded so well in easy
failure. Rose hung
and haunted. Winner.

Lover. Willow cello lover.
Anyone is. Find me
so old in morning.

No wonder agony. Body
whittled infinite
detail. Not by hand.

Lonely art of cutting away
what's also right. Feral,
and all my life.

Quick night reverses
nothing but slow
brings light. By accident.

Parallax

I

Excluding genitalia,
What is a man?
A little boy all grown. A reverse neverland.

What is a woman?
Easier. She's a cipher, she hasn't been
decided yet. Also she's a queen.

If you're not here, you're not necessarily
there. Not yet.
Brown dwarfs are those sad bodies too bright

to be planets but too cool
to be stars. They lean into stars, nestled
and wary. To burn or to crust, both crisp

choices, but for this dead androgyne,
there's only Pandora's squeezebox, locked.
Come closer, toward the light.

II

Kitten, six-pack, magnolia,
a goose behind a desk. Please let us
find ourselves a suckhole forever.

I could never stop. I would never start again.
Bacon, bucket, queerbaby,
I am so big I will not smell you.

We all know Gaea and Apollo
never made it with each other. Territorial.
Brushfire. I have already expelled you,

and now have the luxury of knowing you
differently: perversely leonine
with a hex on your light-haired belly,

and swinging,
first dangerous, then fragile, then repulsive,
then repulsed.

Cinema Poisoning

I will be your first, your thirst, your third.
I'll cramp up boxy, I will starlet out
in roads of light, or crimes, or words.
My second coming would not be allowed
unless your masokismet lifts her skirts.
So I will hold you flush against the glass.
Your voice & eye are muscle & they hurt
like prodigy too soft or quick in class.

My double agent, you would never ask
my miracles of sass & light to train
the athletes of seduction in the crass
voluptuary sciences like rain.

The sex & chess & cello fever's gone
from your myopic trust, my Avalon.

Postfeminism

There are two kinds of people, soldiers and women,
as Virginia Woolf said. Both for decoration only.

Now that is too kind. It's technical: virgins and wolves.
We have choices now. Two little girls walk into a bar,

one orders a shirley temple. Shirley Temple's pimp
comes over and says you won't be sorry. She's a fine

piece of work but she don't come cheap. Myself, I'm
in less fear of predators than of walking around

in my mother's body. That's sneaky, that's more
than naked. Let's even it up: you go on fuming in your

gray room. I am voracious alone. Blank and loose,
metallic lingerie. And rare black-tipped cigarettes

in a handmade basket case. Which of us weaves
the world together with a quicker blur of armed

seduction: your war-on-thugs, my body stockings.
Ascetic or carnivore. Men will crack your glaze

even if you leave them before morning. Pigs
ride the sirens in packs. Ah, flesh, technoflesh,

there are two kinds of people. Hot with mixed
light, drunk with insult. You and me.

Wrongbodied

Like this baby boy standing there on the corner,
hand in jean pocket, lolly too like a cigarette;
even small is too big for him. And winter
too small for the smallest snow, so there is none.
None is too many for me. If I had any, I'd leave
them all. A baby so cynical in his wrongbody is not
loveable, but past love. I am. God, if it were
you I'd change you, as if you'd need changing
and you do. God, if it were you I'd say, *"Pick me, God."*
Next corner, God, me.

Arachnolescence

I see I have so quickly endeared you to my dazzled fray
of bedpan. With a stealth hand on my breastbone,
I've pilfered the last gangrene remedy, honey-wax fiber,
from my neighbor all century and I've bullied you
into a few cramps yourself. Give me drug
of terrifying strength or I will become it.

Love me in my strict empire of phantom pain,
in my wiliest contempt for all that is mere fever
and sweat, strain and maculate, florid and maternal,
decent and plain. I want theater, the domain
of intoxicated grief. And spifflicated louts are we,
absolute gourmands of the ugliest meal.

I have a radium of the soul, a petulant amputation, eight!
A poultice for you, my arachno-demigod, wacky and skeptical.
A promise of loot and skulduggery for all your children.

I've won the tourniquet, I've devastated toddlers
in the height of their podlike fashion, in their pink-naped
heaven of Erasmus and his near-wife, Chlamydia.
Give me five years, lovers, I will give you the ancient torture
device constructed of kisses, in the glum transfusion
of crisp, lichen climate with rectangular erotics.

I will kill you with the blistering foods of a Crimean war,
sluiced with a dura mater's soldier-ration of tiny
moistures, in this temple of my tryst with the daughter
of the red god's red dog. I will solder you to the Krsna
of ironworks and most bellicose dementia. Give me liberty
or give me everything you've ever loved.

Stop me, my ancient history, as you always have,
before I poison my own sleep with the wanderlust
of this my stardom in the galaxy of worms and toxic ability.

The Question and Its Mark

May I cast a spell on the many swans of Leda,
making at last one spastic blizzard in spring
with only enough divine mania to take one
blinding day from her?

The godbirds and their scopophilia
keep her open for view and review, with ever
new speculum and never the elegant jewelry
of stigmata or a heart of quartz.

May I give her only one death? Can we live if she
lies closed in a single final pose, no syphilitic
autopsy or cygnet interrogation?
May I mark her prophecy,

her presence in the very air, with a single
gargoyle on the streetside wall on a place
of worship, finally allowed inside if only by
disappearing into the stones?

Leda possessed a pair of knees that also bent
in prayer. I ask of you only what she asked for there.

[*III*]

Project for

a Fainting

Project for a Fainting

Oh, yes, the rain is sorry. Unfemale, of course, the rain is
with her painted face still plain and with such pixel you'd never see

it in the pure freckling, the lacquer of her. The world
is lighter with her recklessness, a handkerchief so wet it is clear.

To you. My withered place, this frumpy home (nearer
to the body than to evening) miserable beloved. I lie tender

and devout with insomnia, perfect on the center pillow past
midnight, sick with the thought of another year

of waking, solved and happy, it has never been this way! Believe
strangers who say the end is close for what could be closer?

You are my stranger and see how we have closed. On both ends.
Night wets me all night, blind, carried.

And watermarks. The plough of the rough on the slick,
love, a tendency toward fever. To break. To soil.

Would I dance with you? Both forever and rather die.
It would be like dying, yes. Yes I would.

I have loved the slaking of your forgetters, your indifferent
hands on my loosening. Through a thousand panes of glass

not all transparent, and the temperature.
I felt that. What you say is not less than that.

Perfect Ending

Be anti-grandmother in your little black box.
The hinges must be real gold, and wing-shaped.

Increase your interest in Chronos, your chromosomes
like heirloom silver in their silky drawers.

Return all your gifts and melt alone,
naked in a new polytropic isle.

In other words, trade your ugly juvenilia

for sweet Saturnalia,
infinitely.

Supply the weapons for Ulysses and Odysseus,
fighting for the use of their name.

Convince everyone you are qualified,

a fine fattened pig

with your degree in Endstopography,
your success in plant school.

Shut up, in everyear, in the negative mirror,
in the absolute no light.

The Lamp Garden

Neither electric nor flame, unimaginable sunlight or plagiarist moon.
Small bulbs of desire, like uprooted tulips pulled open on a whim
   by a tongue.
With colored or clear shades to temper the glee. The spring glee
   of lamps.

Where you can sit or even lie reading newly soft and gentle pages
   that flirt
rather than glare. Play chess and be undisturbed by your partner's
   too-bold
queen. Play free of the strange cast of eye that makes such a game
   too eerie to
play in usual environments. The naked strategy.

You can balance your checkbook in such a way that if you peer
   closely at the
tiny pages, you can see the imprinted numbers you made weeks
   ago even with
the hastiest of pens. You remember what shape the headache was
   that made
you forget to record your little life.

As you start to write a page it doesn't appear appallingly blank,
   something is

soothing, encouraging, like steam on the bathroom mirror that
    wishes you to
draw your face on it. You can tell, when a sentence is hard to
    write, whether it
is because there's a knot in your throat or in the tree before it was
    your tablet.

The lamp garden is outside, surrounded by city blasts and honks
    and sirens,
wails and guffaws, rumbles and shuffles. You don't hear it, because
    the right
light cancels the wrong sound. It's synesthesia in our favor.

Unlike other places, it doesn't have an exact address or cross-
    street, but like
other places, if you need to get there, you will find it. I work at the
    lamp
garden. I receive no salary, only gratuity.

I have read the same book, at work, over and over again, because
    each time it
is so vastly different. On the green plaid couch or on the six-foot
    black wood
executioner's chair, on the tin can bed.

The story is never old, like a day at home with an unpredictable
    lover. It starts
where Sarah wonders if time begins when she wakes up or when
    everybody
else does. Her question leaves as she faces a grumpy breakfast
with me.

Because the cream is spotty in the coffee, the sleepy fury that is
    adorable.
Because my angel is irritable with loveable hairs stuck to her
    cheeks from a
sideways night of unconscious travel. The hairs are like tickets.

The middle, where Sarah runs through rainy streets with only
    galoshes and a
plastic slicker on (I imagine it is clear), finds me swampy and
    kissed over,
running to where the me in her has gone to, a perfect kind of
    alone.

At this point in the book it helps me to move to a discreet section
    of the lamp
garden, where rice-paper screens filter the light the way eyebrows
    kindly

keep rain from your eyes, even in dry seasons, but only in certain
    directions.

Where tatami mats blithely ignore your slippery body and appear
    unburdened
when another slides beside it. Her bare feet became strangers, déjà
    vu beings
that ring a bell on somebody else's cow. Beings you end up sitting
    on in your
own ignorant love of the body.

Her feet were so sensitive, this is what happened as I touched
    them. Each little
toe as I caressed it was, believe me it's true, a child in a large farm
    family,
unscathed by too many buildings but heavily touched by wind.

The oldest daughter with the big face, the much smaller boy with
    pitchfork.
And as I approached each one, I was the beloved town-folk visitor
    coming to
bestow my special gift on each milky young thing.

Each delicately wrapped and gratefully received gift, in a sober
    country
mouse/city mouse ceremony, was a handling involving more than
    chapped
fingers and the relief of a rag doll or a bottle of lilac water, a
    slingshot or a
paddle-game. Exchanging fevers of disproportionate loss.

But I skipped a child. Ignored him and went on to the baby who
    curled in
delight. I saw the small towheaded boy, head bowed politely. I
    look up at my
love, I have somehow missed her fourth toe, her curvy one. I went
    back and
showered the little one, keeper of balance, edge of her being, with
    gifts.

Where the light pierces through your world, it lives underneath.
    In the god-
given vertigo, it wrestles you down. In the lamp garden, I will
    forever keep
reading this book. It keeps my place, like love or a father, it gives
    me away.

Ten Jennies

My house is just big enough to fit most
of the Ten Jennies. At parties they share
chairs with the one Lola, Furtina and me.

Some Jennies are performers and exclude
Other Jennies in their work but several
Jennies are absorbers and soak themselves

back in. I love to cut the hair of each one,
lucky sharp points where each of them ends
in a hundred thousand foxy ways—ending

oneself isn't dying it's cutting, it's washing.
I wash ten cups wet from the lips of the Ten
Jennies, and two for Furtina and me (Lola

gets no cup she's a plant, a kind of spy).
A dozen hail-breaded oysters, warm liquor.
Delineating. We cut the stems of our Jennies,

We swirled their liquid and watched their faces.
And then a subtle morning comes and floury
light slims us around our sleep. We pressed

ourselves to the high outer rim of summer
and now never any Jennies.

Calling Her Home

She died before I was born but that didn't stop us.
She'd come wearing a certain hat,
she'd say my name with such salt!

She called me Mary. Or Anna, or sometimes Bijou
when I was very hungry.
She believed me to be many,

and I became whichever, and came whenever
she called. My rooms were small,
you see, I was ashamed,

and lined the walls with mirror. She was urgent
for lightness, the blue height
of moonbaths on the roof,

heels slung up off the ground, dresses weightless
at the hem. *Do not think
of flying above, think*

of cities suspended. Oh, now I am embellishing.
Making her up, deepening,
shading, brushing down.

The first finishing touch smiling into a paper
to blot her lips. Of these papers
she made me a dress I wore

on the inside. The red marks smeared. To make
is to mark: *When I saw
you, Mary, I chose my body.*

I told you she died before I was born, did she tell you
that lie, too? Her living, looking-
glass body is here, heard,

as mine is. We never sleep, not soundly, for we can't
breathe a hair of this.
We live with slivered faces.

The tiniest room is ours and has no door. You see her hat
flying off, her mouth opening
in surprise to find herself here.

Musée

I've been so lovingly breathed into it appears I can't move.
I've been stuck on.

A remission of stopping, honey-frozen, gecko mid-pushup.
Astronomy's attractions run on light and eye.

If I smiled, I'd crack. Fake heartbreak. Zero depth of throat
and pussy no intricacy,

how could it? Fever 103, my nothing! Imagine being real
only because only one

lonely one thought you so. You make it so. Like acting
but no voice only lines.

Thick makeup as thick as I am. I leave and become a kind
of nefertiti when you look down

at your knees. While you think are my knees as oily
I have been her,

bodiless and as such, truly naked. When I am only all thoughts
I can move

elsewhere, pure vessel, empty of body water but spilling
proud kinesis unmoored.

When you look at me again I can't think. I've gone
spread to the surface.

It's like a privacy. When you think of lobsters you see shell
and you understand only eat.

When you see a bust of ancient, broken personage, someone
without a name is running faster.

You Love, You Wonder

You love a woman and you wonder where she goes all night in
    some tricked-
out taxicab, with her high heels and her corset and her big, fat
    mouth.

You love how she only wears her glasses with you, how thick
and cow-eyed she swears it's only ever you she wants to see.

You love her, you want her very ugly. If she is lovely big, you
    want her
scrawny. If she is perfect lithe, you want her ballooned, a
    cosmonaut.

How not to love her, her bouillabaisse, her orangina. When you
    took her
to the doctor the doctor said, "Wow, look at that!" and you were
    proud,

you asshole, you love and that's how you are in love. Any expert,
    observing
human bodies, can see how she's exceptional, how she ruins us
    all.

But you really love this woman, how come no one can see this?
Everyone must
become suddenly very clumsy at recognizing beauty if you are to
keep her.

You don't want to lose anything, at all, ever. You want her sex
depilated, you
want everyone else not blind, but perhaps paralyzed, from the eyes
down.

You wonder where she goes all night. If she leaves you, you will
know
everything about love. If she's leaving you now, you already know
it.

Voluptuary

Normal love begs for kink. Loving wrong
is twisted and hair, the hair of blood-timed
mammals and damsels in paintings curls
subversively without effort.

And espionage of flesh roots in the dirt
of the heart. Vinegar love floods the tongue
with a uriny fire and who argues? Sour aunts.
In lovers' mouths, only saccharine is unholy.

And if my sister married now then I will
wed wonder, I will seek blunder,
and wifely be naked for a throttled,
verging slumber slit with: love is losing.

If you haven't known the true faulty
pleasure of half-beauty, the sublime uncomely,
dreamt without vision two hot marble arches
round your vague orca trumpet of a thigh,

then why would you love me? And how does
fever break without liquid, without spilling?
What woman cannot speak of strumpets? Who
has struck the head of lust without a strain?

Where is the mark, the dark, the brain?
I want terror only listening for the shallows
in the shame. Like dancers, elasticize time
for the sake of the body. And what body?

Blister, wizen. It's worth it and it's night.
Who wants pretty, when pretty is plain
and the heart is gnarled and the fullsacked
forest of being lost is home?

Forest where we love the beast surprising.
Anticipated fetish like missing toes. Or a thick,
dark, hairy heart, full to pluck or comb.
Or old. Where is the old, old lover;

finally ripe enough to fall without falling?
What is blossoming
when the darker sun inside feeds
the silence of starker stars?

Mistress Formika

In temple city, in this tight lighthouse of rare women,
my falling goggles stinging in the lemon juice
of all my watching, where even your synthetic

hairs are generous, yielding to a stiff ritual, perfect with your
gynecoid East Village supersmirk. That smarts!
This performance of thighs blessed with an excruciating

unnatural talent for the part. For the parting.
And the pupils, we, and the lashes, all yours, observe
the rules of tragedy-in-sumptuous-fabrics, loving but strict,

in fact bullying, my god the backwatching and the switchblade!
And all imaginary: the spell a queen casts on her bee, a lover will
let herself be made up in orange for the beloved, but yours

is a sweeter exercise, twistier. Thank you, for shaking, for
who hasn't forgotten how to use her diva-noodle?
Can this be too much pleasure in one so smart, debauched

and thin? So far beyond wondering we have fallen
into quarreling, braided evening feelers in hand,
with this dark stallion blindness, too close to the fence to jump

it clean. You, both gate and barrier to the hearth and breast
of Eve and Adam's apple orchard. And I stumble over
strange broken pieces strewn everywhere, what's the damage?

Is it you sleeping in the grass, dear with a cheeky bliss,
pale and mournful? The delicious no-secret plain and defused,
genitalia quiet and ripe, the gorgon of your hair loved off

and lying guilty where you tossed it,
by the broken fence, firewood for a home too well built
for such arsonists of the flesh to resist.

Panopticon

My bedroom window can be seen from the viewing deck
of the World Trade Center. I've seen it.
What I saw?

My roommate experimenting with my vibrator.
She looked lovely through sheer curtains
on my creamy bed. Is she thinking of me?

I am thinking of her and I left bread crumbs on the telepath.
She can feel it, my seeing, even through a trance of fog.
I've lit her with it.

It is her blindfold, her sweet curse, her ration
of privacy spilled like flour as she imagines
the miraculous bread is rising.

I decided on three possible reactions:

To keep watching her and, when I go home, to mention
the strange vision I had, describing
what I saw in detail.

To feed the telescope with quarter
after quarter, and read a book while the time ticks.
I have been blessed with seeing, as with a third eye,
without the compulsive mimesis of appearing. The luxury
of an octopus is never using any legs for walking.

Or, to stay home with my own
pair of binoculars, in the dark, watching whoever is
watching me, watch me.

Ever

Where, swift and wool in going?
Fell always wishing like this.

Tomorrow, want less and hunger bigger.
Fewer terror but stronger, staggered.

Taken heart outside to dry.
Rain surprise and ruined.

Silver cold and stops the swelling.
Why hurts from other body?

Why photo soothes with flat?
Salt soaks blood tender.

Brighten flesh in slap.
With word, not flood silent.

Not leave and take me
nowhere, swift and wool in going.

Sleptember

I love the quiet but I carve out its motives,

one by one always more. You have in a photo

of flowerheads, a squabbly roaring. In a gaze,

many bibles semifluid in endless revision.

The sweat of leisure sounds like an argument,

but glad. Can you help me pack my whole

prairie in a handbox? There's a tiny sumo

wrestling in New England and in its veinstains,

the wily silence of a croning: at fifty,

each woman secretly pleased.

Why is the width between ovaries a hand?

Will you point everything you have

that smacks of blue towards the soil

and reflect it upwards? Is that how we have

such a sky so supercilious with its kindling

and spin? I swam a terrible night swim

through pillars of gel, each thick translucence

like a leg heavy with sequatic shadows, and once

everything is submerged in water nothing is wet.

Sound is a melon bowled under you.

Why sing when before you weren't singing?

All your years of deep, hot thinking shrink

to one tiny Wildean gnomy quipster,

"Vladimir is glad I'm here" and whatnot.

Why an excess of hands to hold open and prove

empty in perfect bowl form? In my most rare

of dances, what I call "The Cuisinart,"

I display this tender power. Used up

our uselessness, haven't we? But sometimes a can

opener weasels its way cutely into your house

of vague peppermint uglies. It's some perverse

test of depth for us flatheads—it's a share-tactic—

to help us get naked in the brain. To help us step

up to the realm of the new uninvisible.

These cakey spectacles are such a throwgloom,

aren't they? Why only one mind so as to

have to change it often? And often with a holstered

silencer on the future perfect literature smuggled

forever out of your implicit country.

Illumine

I open her dark diary,
lotus and teasing where
we're bound together. Witch's
book of vim and bliss.
The spell-cracked spine.
All mine.

Her hands have the acidity
of a whisper, carving
like stone on softer stone.
The sound is sweet
with Sisyphus. Oh,
my scavenger's daughter.

I know the orifice,
the edges of the absence,
by the tracing of her very
tips, her erasing. Straining
me pure through
the lakeshadow of her.

Replacing fog with light
shelter, the morning throat.

It's a small place.
I am less than one.
More than two. I laugh
at the ways to count a person.

I'm a sliver till she looks
through. A good book
gives you secrets but keeps
one. The mirror knows
how edgy its own silhouette is.
This book keeps me.

Now, sable or silver aubade
silent at last. The story
locked in the rubbing
of hands through stone cell
walls to wellwater.
This nulla swells

the netherworlds. Bring me
closer and teach me
closing. Teach me losing.
Each morning, at leaving,

something must be torn.
I must rise to open the blinds.

How light tears, sears,
the body. And seals
in its impossible script.

Interior with Sudden Joy

[*after a painting by Dorothea Tanning*]

To come into my room is to strike strange.
My plum velvet pillow & my hussy spot
the only furniture.

Red stripes around my ankles, tight
as sisters. We are maybe fourteen, priceless
with gooseflesh.

Our melon bellies, our mouths of tar. Us four:
my mud legged sister, my bunched-up self,
the dog & the whirligig just a prick on the eye.

We are all sewn in together, but the door is open.
The book is open too. You must write in red
like Jesus and his friends.

Be my other sister, we'll share a mouth.
We'll split the dress
down the middle, our home, our Caesarian.

When the Bishop comes he comes
diagonal, from the outside, & is a lie.
He comes to bless us all with cramps,

mole on the chin that he is,
to bring us the red something,
a glow, a pumping.

Not softly a rub with loincloth
& linseed. More of a beating,
with heart up the sleeve.

He says, *The air in here is tight & sore*
but punctured, sudden, by a string quartet.
We are! In these light-years we've wrung a star.

I am small for my age.
Child of vixenwood, lover of the color olive
and its stain.

I live to leave, but I never either.
One leg is so long we can all walk it.
Outside is a thousand bitten skins

and civilization its own murder of crows.
I am ever stunned,
seduced whistle-thin

& hot with home. Breathless with
mercury, columbine. Come, let us miss
another wintertime.

Acknowledgments

Grateful acknowledgement is made to the editors of the following journals in which some of these poems have appeared, or are forthcoming.

Interior with Sudden Joy, Parallax, and *Afterlife, Her Empty Dress* appeared in *Paris Review.*

Jouissance, Fetish: The Historical Orphan, and *Vapor through Various Satins* appeared in *Western Humanities Review.*

Letter to the Crevice Novice, Perfect Ending, Rosarium, Middle, Your Name on It, Postfeminism, The Question and Its Mark, and *Thirteenth Summer* appeared in *Chelsea.*

Still Life, with Gloxinia and *Your One Good Dress* appeared in *The Yale Review.*

Fortune, Project for a Fainting, Mistress Formika, and *What's Uncanny* appeared in *Boston Review.*

Thank you to Mitsuko Shaughnessy, Bob Shaughnessy, the Shaughnessy family, the Higa family, and the Damans for all the love near and far. To my sister, Lisa, and Steve. To the incomparable Dorothea Tanning, for her friendship and wisdom and for her work which has changed and informed mine immeasurably. To Bill Wadsworth and Jonathan Galassi, for their shocking belief in me. To the Academy of

American Poets. To Richard Howard, for honoring me with his attention, intelligence, and heart. To Lucie Brock-Broido, who with brilliant teaching helped shape this book mysteriously. Billy Collins, Mark Doty, Alfredo DiPalchi, J. D. McClatchy, Sophie Cabot Black, Richard Foerster, Wendy Brown, Judith Butler, Helene Moglen, and Carla Freccero; also for their true believing. Timothy Donnelly, Lynn Melnick, Mark Wunderlich, Merrill Feitell, Jamie Mirabella, Mike Albo, Monica De La Torre, Jeni Saunders, Michelle Elligott, Liz Spencer, Cynthia Yahia, Sayeeda Clarke, Ronan Culhane, Louise Dunne, Carrie Barnes, Scott Zieher, Ravi Rajakumar, Laura White, Trista Sordillo, Saije Bashaw and Lucia Matioli, Al and Joan Gauthier: each for their crucial friendships, encouragement, and sense of family. To Cris Beam and Robin Goldman, for their constant and unexplainable love. And to my dear Tina.

I also wish to thank Dorothea Tanning for allowing me to use the titles of two of her paintings, *Interior with Sudden Joy* and *Project for a Fainting*; the MacDowell Colony, New York University's International Center for Advanced Studies, and the Oscar M. Ruebhausen Commission of the Greenwall Foundation for their generous support.